80 YEARS AGO BACK IN 1944

MAJOR WORLD LEADERS

UK- PM WINSTON CHURCHILL

US- PRESIDENT FRANKLIN D. ROOSEVELT

RUSSIA/SOVIET UNION - JOSEPH STALIN

ITALY - PM BENITO MUSSOLINI

GERMANY - ADOLF HITLER

CANADA -PM WILLIAM LYON MCKENZIE KING

SOUTH AFRICA - PM FIELD MARSHALL JAN CHRISTIAAN SMUTS

MEXICO - MANUEL AVILA CAMACHO

JAPAN - FUMIMARO KONOE / HIDEKI TOLO

1944 World Population

2.3 BILLION

Britain population

48.2 MILLION

2024 World Population

8.1 BILLION

Britain population

68.34 MILLION

Born 1944
80 & Fabulous

Michael Douglas
- Born 25th September
- American Actor & Producer
- 2 Academy Awards, 5 Golden Globe Awards and a Primetime Emmy Awards to name a few.

George Lucas

- Born 14th May
- American Filmmaker
- Creator of Star Wars & Indiana Jones

Diana Ross

- Born March 26st
- American Singer & Actress
- Found fame as lead singer of the Supremes
- They remain the best selling girls group of all time

Jimmy Page

- Born January 9th
- OBE
- English Musician
- Lead guitarist for Yardbirds and founder of rock band Led Zeppelin

Joe Cocker

- Born May 20th
- OBE
- English singer/Songwriter

Roger Daltrey

- Born March 1st
- English Singer and Actor
- Best known for his work as lead singer of rock band The Who

Barry White

- Born September 12th
- American singer/Song writer and Producer

Oscars

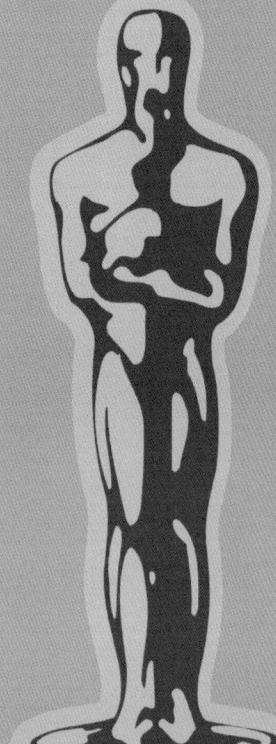

Best Actor

Paul Lukas

Watch on the Rhine

Box Office

2.5 million USD

Best Actress

Jennifer Jones

The Song of the Bernadette

Box Office

5 million USD

Average cost of living 1944

Average House £550 - In todays money thats £27,947
Average Salary £195 - In todays money thats £9,908
Average Car price £310 - In todays money thats £15,752
Average food shop £0.39 - In todays money thats £19.82

Food Shopping

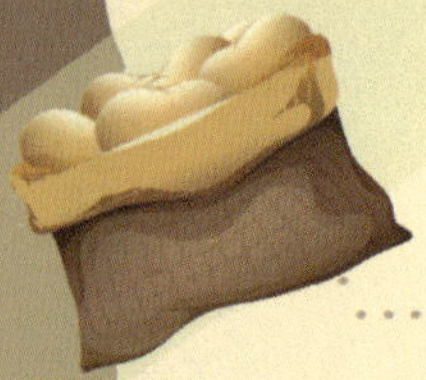

FLOUR 1.5KG £0.03 - £1.52 today

BREAD 1 LOAF £0.01 - 51p today

SUGAR 1KG £0.04 - £2.03 today

MILK 1PT £0.07 - £3.56 today

BUTTER 250G £0.04 - £2.03 today

CHEESE 400G £0.05 - £2.54 today

POTATOES 2.5KG £0.03 - £1.52 today

BACON 400G £0.12 - £6.10 today

- Approximately 70-80 million people died in World War II, most of them from four countries - Russia, China, Germany & Poland. The majority of victims were women and children, numbering between 50 and 55 million.

- Adolph Hitler's nephew, William Hitler, served in the US Navy during World War II.

- During World War II, Americans adopted the name Liberty Steak in order to avoid the sound of the German word hamburger.

- The discovery of silly putty occurred during a General Electric Engineer's attempt to make synthetic rubber.
- Copper and nickel were both needed for the war effort during World War II. During 1943, zinc was coated on low-grade steel pennies. Previously, copper-based bronze was used. The U.S. Mint resumed minting copper pennies in 1944. In 1943, 40 copper pennies were accidentally created and quickly became collectibles.

Welcome to the world -1944

Mary
Barbara
Patricia
Carol
Linda
Judith
Betty
Nancy
Sandra
Carolyn

10 Most Popular Boys & Girls Names

James
Robert
John
William
Richard
Charles
David
Thomas
Ronald
Donald

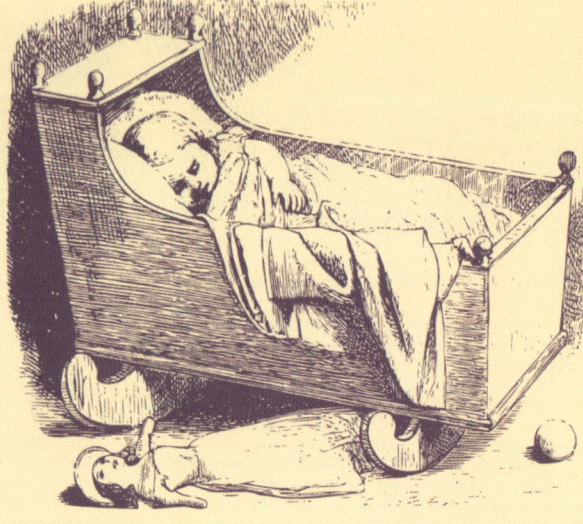

Books published 1944

- How to Stop Worrying and Start Living (Dale Carnegie Books)
- Ficciones by Jorge Luis Borges
- Forever Amber by Kathleen Winsor
- Take Me with You by Catherine Ryan Hyde
- Nada by Carmen Laforet
- The Road to Serfdom by Friedrich A. Hayek
- The Hundred Dresses by Eleanor Estes
- No Exit by Jean-Paul Sartre
- Five Run Away Together (Famous Five, #3)

Books & Publishing

There is a lesser-known victim of WWII: books and the publishing industry. Despite the devastating effects on the country, the impact on the publishing industry is less well known. A reduced workforce, censorship restrictions, and paper shortages plagued the industry. The rationing of paper took place between 1940 and 1949. The publishing industry faced significant challenges in order to remain strong. Despite this, the publishing industry persevered, and many of these books are still considered classics today. As the war progressed, entertainment and distraction became increasingly important. Contrary to this, the ability to supply was limited. Books and magazines had poor margins and typefaces, and the industry was unable to meet consumer demands. However, local libraries' patronage reached an all-time high as a result of it.

Films

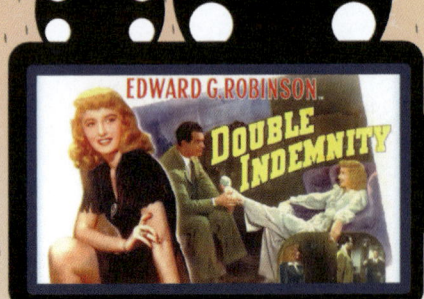

A Los Angeles insurance representative lets an alluring housewife seduce him into a scheme of insurance fraud and murder that arouses the suspicion of his colleague, an insurance investigator.

A police detective falls in love with the woman whose murder he is investigating.

Young love and childish fears highlight a year in the life of a turn-of-the-century family.

Films 1944

Cinemas during the War

After the declaration of war in 1939, cinemas were immediately closed. After a few weeks, the government realized people needed entertainment, so they reopened the theaters. Cinema attendance soared after 1942. The number of admissions to cinemas reached just over 1.5 billion in 1944. During the war, going to the cinema was one of the nation's favorite leisure activities. As a method of educating and informing people, it proved to be effective.

- **Double Indemnity** starring Fred MacMurray, Barbara Stanwyck.
- **Laura** starring Gene Tierney, Dana Andrews, Clifton Webb, Vincent Price
- **Meet Me In St. Louis** starring Judy Garland, Margaret O'Brien, Mary Astor
- **Henry V** starring Laurence Olivier, Robert Newton, Leslie Banks, Felix Aylmer
- **To Have and Have Not** starring Humphrey Bogart, Lauren Bacall
- **The Miracle of Morgan's Creek** starring Eddie Bracken, Betty Hutton
- **Arsenic and Old Lace** starring Cary Grant, Priscilla Lane, Raymond Massey
- **Hail the Conquering Hero** Sterling Eddie Bracken, Ella Raines,
- **Murder, My Sweet** starring Dick Powell, Claire Trevor, Anne Shirley, Otto Kruger

Music

At Kohima, when 27-year-old Forces' Sweetheart Vera Lynn arrived on the Burma front line in 1944, she provided troops thousands of miles from home with just the tonic they needed. Vera Lynn, 27, arrived at her bamboo hut in Bawli Bazar after driving through swirling jungle mist for eight hours. She was touched to find a bouquet of handpicked flowers waiting for her. When she sang for them, powered by searchlight batteries and with a pistol in her hand, it was a sign of defiance more powerful than any weapon.

BBC & Music

British soldiers listened to German radio stations during the war to hear dance music, so the BBC had to adapt. There was conflict in the process of adapting. Dance music was played more frequently by the BBC, but censorship was severe. George Formby and Gracie Fields were heavily played on the radio in an effort to preserve the upbeat tone which the BBC believed had contributed to the victory in World War I. The most famous soloist of the era was Vera Lynn, whose popularity led her to be referred to as "the sweetheart of the armed forces".

On March 1, 1904, Glenn Miller (Alton Glen Miller) was born in Clarinda, Iowa. Before and during World War II, Miller was a notable American big band founder, owner, conductor, composer, "ace" arranger, trombone player, and recording artist while in the military. Glenn Miller and His Orchestra have been considered one of the most successful big bands of the 20th century and the big band era generally.

Sports

Wartime League

In England, the Wartime League replaced the suspended Football League during World War II. In these years, the FA Cup was excluded, resulting in the Football League War Cup.

In the wake of the German invasion of Poland in 1939 and the British declaration of war against Nazi Germany on 21 September 1939, football games continued, but not in the traditional divisions. Following the establishment of a fifty-mile travelling limit, the Football Association divided the Football League into regional leagues. In the interest of public safety, 8,000 spectators were allowed to attend these games. Eventually, these arrangements were changed, and clubs were allowed to sell tickets at the turnstiles on match days.

Fashion

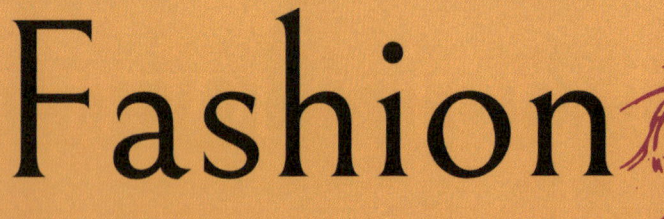

During the first half of the 1940s, the War greatly affected the fashion scene. In the first five years of the war, women and men wore uniforms and rationing defined fashion.

In contrast to flapper girls and Art Deco in the '20s, Hollywood Glamour inspired the '30s with a more conservative approach.

In the early 1940s, silhouettes had a no-nonsense feel, influenced by military style. Playsuits and skirt suits were the most popular styles. Due to rationing, embellishments were lacking. Despite perceived lack of innovation, the military style of the 1940s continues to be admired. Dresses with close-fitting waistbands and utilitarian embellishments flatter the figure while

Fashion

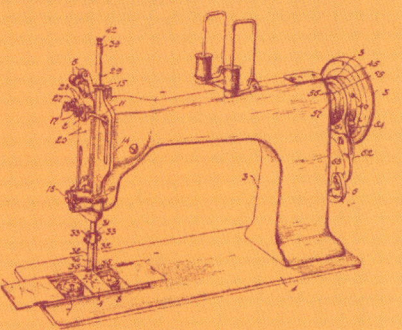

Ration coupon allocation:

In 1941, CC41 became the mandatory marking for utility clothes. For a period of one year, each person received 66 coupons.

- Ladies dress 11 coupons
- Pair of stockings 2 coupons
- Men's shirt 8 coupons
- Footwear - typically 7 coupons

Additional coupons were provided for children who grow out of clothes more quickly. Although you may remember wearing clothes that were a bit too big, your mother always told you "you'll grow into them!"

During the 1940s, jackets could not have pleated backs, metal zippers, or buttons, raglan sleeves, or half belts. The majority of men wore the clothing they wore during the 1930s and early 1940s. Your pre-war suits demonstrated support for the war.

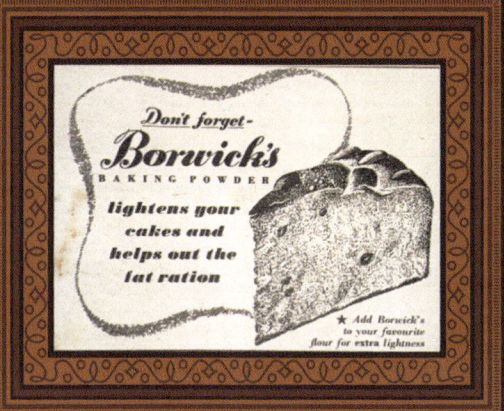

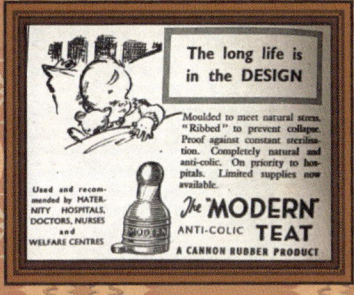

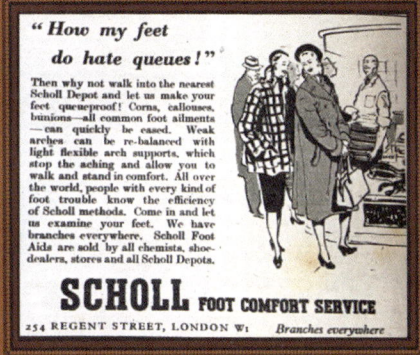

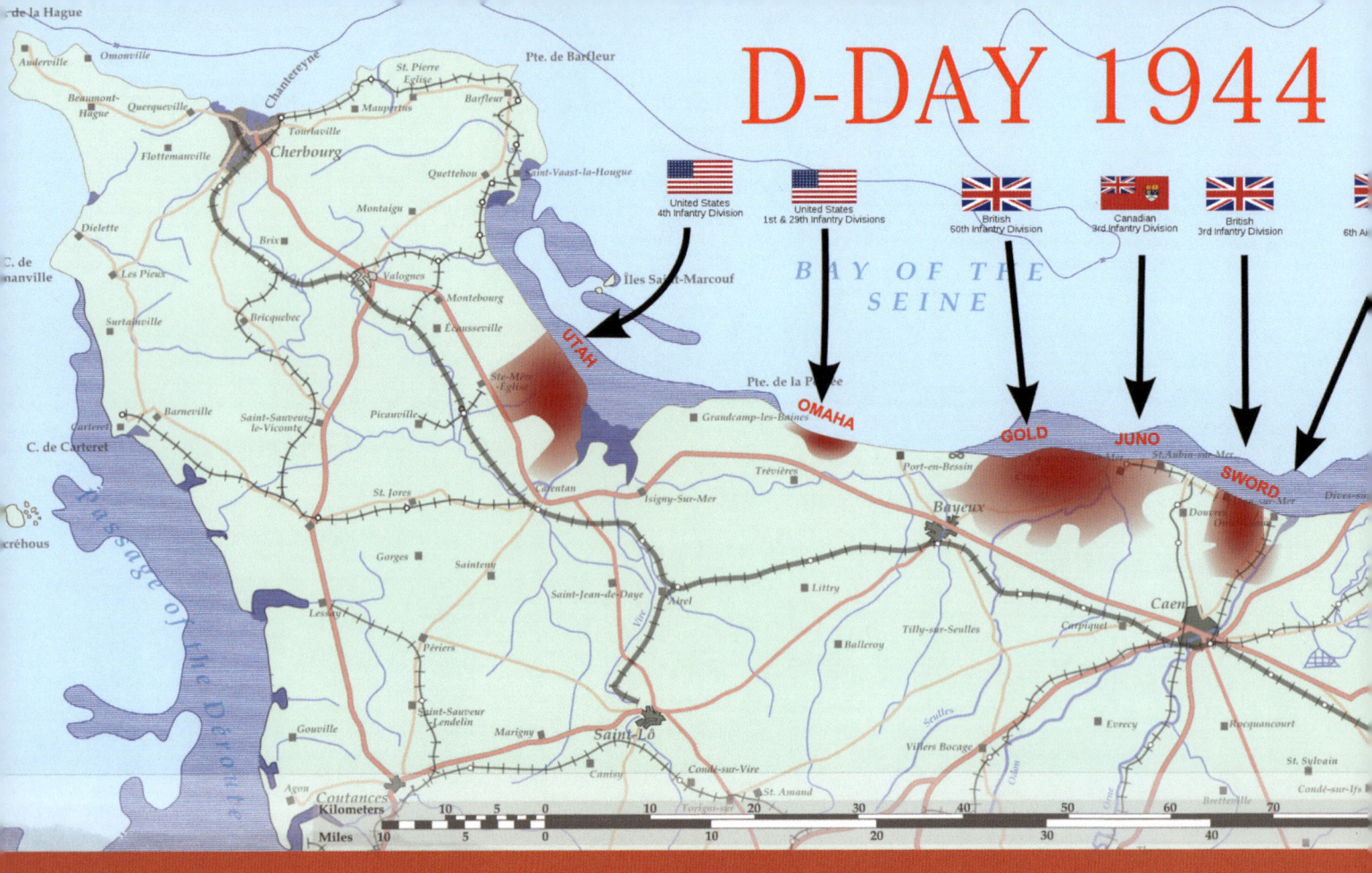

'This operation is planned as a victory, and that's the way it's going to be. We're going down there, and we're throwing everything we have into it, and we're going to make it a success.'

General Dwight D Eisenhower, Supreme Allied Commander in Europe - 1944

June 6th, 1944: In the largest seaborne invasion in history, more than 150,000 Allied troops land on the beaches of Normandy, France. Known as "D-Day," the name and date loom large in the memory of World War II—perhaps second only to December 7th, 1941. These two dates stand on opposite ends of American involvement in the war, and their meaning could not be more different. As a result of D-Day, the Allies were on a decisive path to victory. After taking the Normandy beaches, they pushed back against Axis forces until less than a year later, Germany surrendered. The Normandy invasion resulted in more than 6,000 American casualties, the victory came with significant sacrifice.

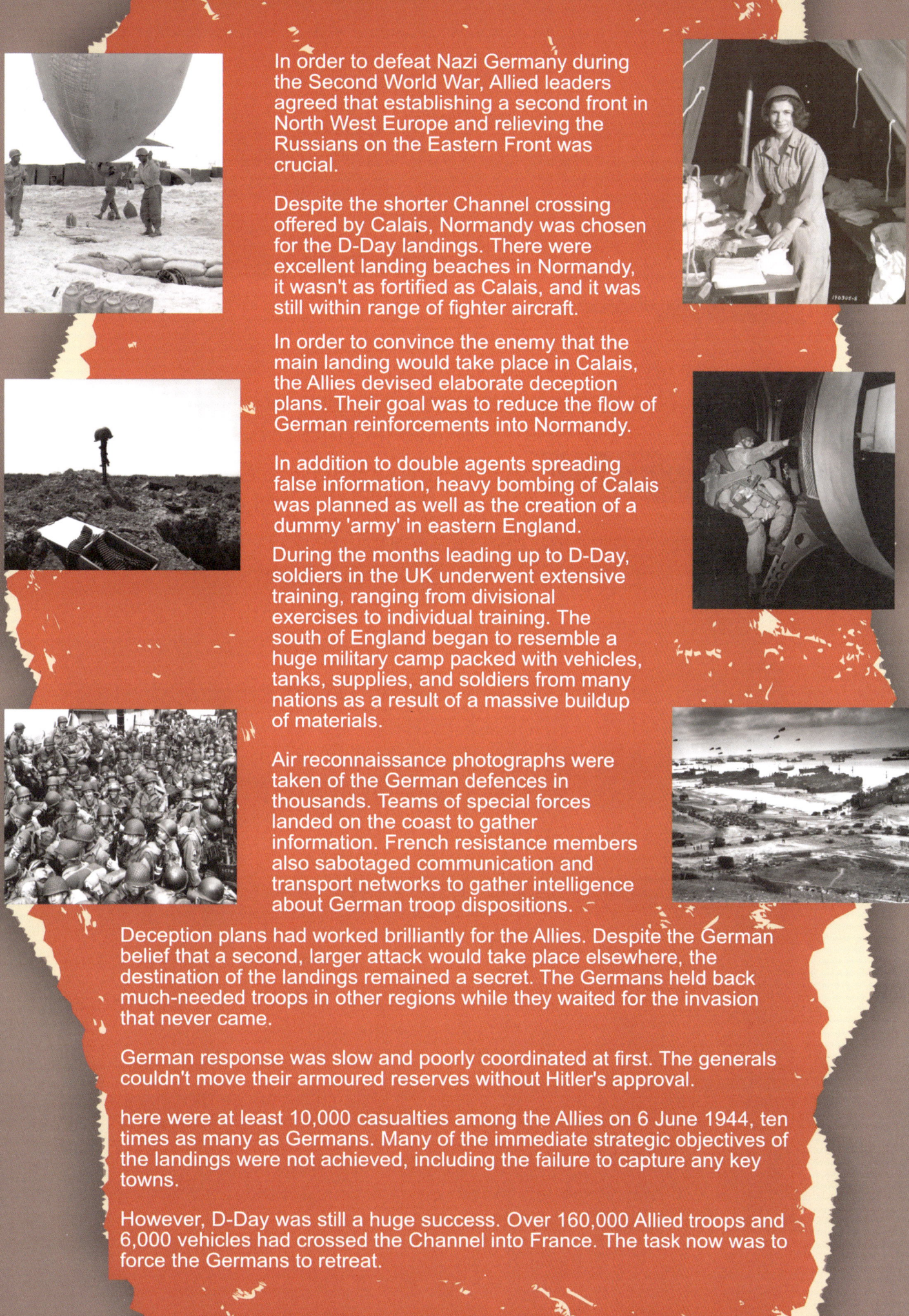

In order to defeat Nazi Germany during the Second World War, Allied leaders agreed that establishing a second front in North West Europe and relieving the Russians on the Eastern Front was crucial.

Despite the shorter Channel crossing offered by Calais, Normandy was chosen for the D-Day landings. There were excellent landing beaches in Normandy, it wasn't as fortified as Calais, and it was still within range of fighter aircraft.

In order to convince the enemy that the main landing would take place in Calais, the Allies devised elaborate deception plans. Their goal was to reduce the flow of German reinforcements into Normandy.

In addition to double agents spreading false information, heavy bombing of Calais was planned as well as the creation of a dummy 'army' in eastern England.

During the months leading up to D-Day, soldiers in the UK underwent extensive training, ranging from divisional exercises to individual training. The south of England began to resemble a huge military camp packed with vehicles, tanks, supplies, and soldiers from many nations as a result of a massive buildup of materials.

Air reconnaissance photographs were taken of the German defences in thousands. Teams of special forces landed on the coast to gather information. French resistance members also sabotaged communication and transport networks to gather intelligence about German troop dispositions.

Deception plans had worked brilliantly for the Allies. Despite the German belief that a second, larger attack would take place elsewhere, the destination of the landings remained a secret. The Germans held back much-needed troops in other regions while they waited for the invasion that never came.

German response was slow and poorly coordinated at first. The generals couldn't move their armoured reserves without Hitler's approval.

here were at least 10,000 casualties among the Allies on 6 June 1944, ten times as many as Germans. Many of the immediate strategic objectives of the landings were not achieved, including the failure to capture any key towns.

However, D-Day was still a huge success. Over 160,000 Allied troops and 6,000 vehicles had crossed the Channel into France. The task now was to force the Germans to retreat.

Wartime Rations

Food rationing was in effect throughout 1944. All of this began on January 8th, 1940 with bacon, ham, sugar, and butter. A rationing program was implemented later in 1940 for meat, tea, margarine, cooking fats, and cheese. The list was again later expanded in to include jam, marmalade, treacle, and syrup. The distribution of eggs was then controlled in June 1941. In August 1941, manual workers received cheese allowances. December 1941 marked the introduction of the national dried milk and vitamin welfare schemes. By mid-1942, everything but vegetables, fruit, fish, and bread was on ration.

Despite the end of the war in 1945, food rationing continued until 4th July 1954, totalling 14 years of food rationing. The end of sweet rationing in 1953 will likely bring back memories of childhood joy (sweet rationing was ended in 1949 but lasted only for months due to feverish demand!).

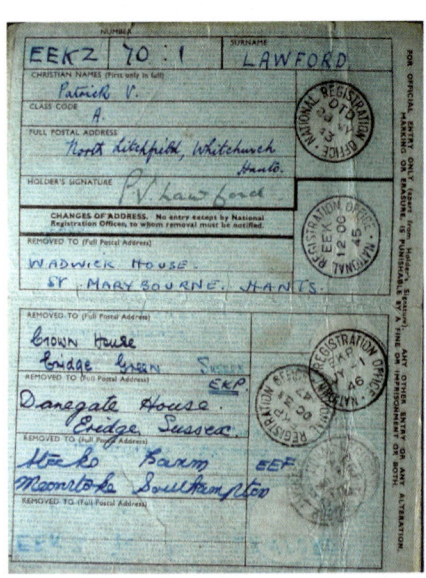

WW2 Rations 1944: per one person (adult)
Butter: 50g (2oz)
Bacon or ham: 100g (4oz)
Margarine: 100g (4oz)
Cooking fat/lard: 100g (4oz)
Sugar: 225g (8oz).
Meat: about 1lb (450g) to 12ozs (350g)
Milk: 3 pints (1800ml) occasionally dropping to 2 pints
Cheese: 2oz (50g) rising to 8oz (225g)
Eggs: 1 fresh egg a week.
Tea: 50g (2oz).
Jam: 450g (1lb) every two months.
Dried eggs: 1 packet (12 eggs) every four weeks.
Sweets & Chocolate: 350g (12oz) every four weeks

Wartime recipe

Wartime Spiced Biscuits

- 225g self raising flour
- 1/4 teaspoon mixed spice
- 1 pinch salt
- 2 tablespoons caster sugar
- 1 dessertspoon dried egg
- 280g margarine
- 2 tablespoons chopped sultanas
- 2 tablespoons raisins
- 1 dessertspoon milk, or more if needed

1. Preheat the oven to 190 C

2. Mix the dried ingredients. Rub the margarine into the mixture until it looks fine breadcrumbs. Add the fruit and then the milk to form a dough. Turn the dough out and roll out to 1cm thickness. Cut into rounds.

3. Bake in the oven for 10 to 15 minutes until golden brown.

It would have been a treat to make these. Margarine is almost three adults' full allowance week. Did you ever get spiced biscuits as a treat? Try some at home and bring back the memories.

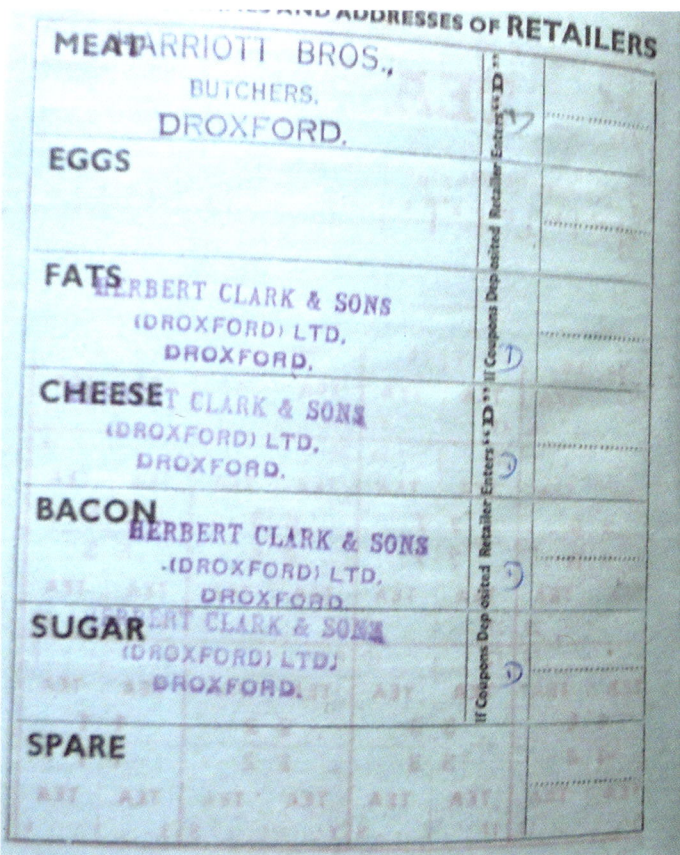
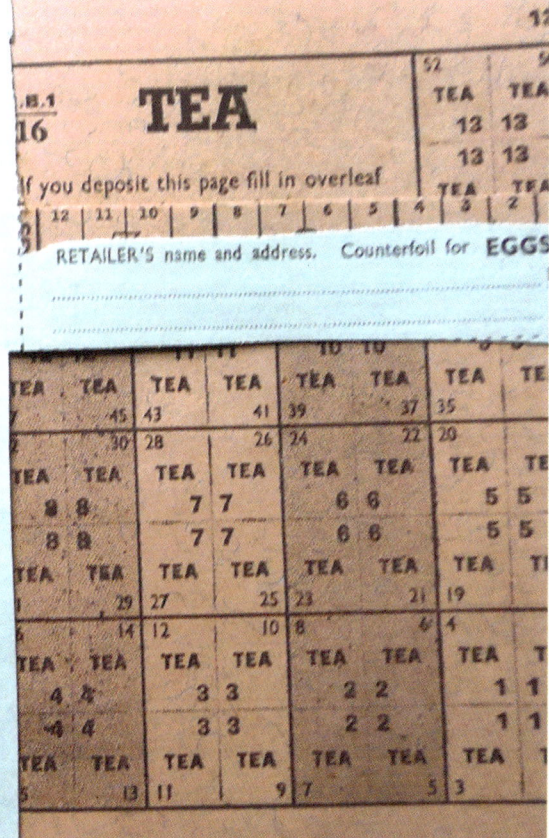

Toys

With World War II in full swing, Britain entered the 1940s under austerity conditions, with shortages of consumer goods and materials. Toys, like other industries, were rationed long after the war ended. Most children used toys passed down from older siblings or made by themselves.

Several firms continued to operate during the war, such as Nicol Toys. Plimpton Engineering, Bayko's manufacturer, used clever substitutions for materials in its construction set. While the aesthetic suffered, neither the company nor its customers were too concerned. From 1941 onwards, toys were no longer produced and all effort was devoted to the war effort, including the production of Wellington bomber parts. In every major city in Britain, children had to endure nightly bombings. When there were no games and toys to distract and entertain them, the impact was severe. Sir William Stephenson, Woolworths' chairman and head of Aircraft Production, was asked to find resources to increase toy production.

He approached Lord Beaverbrook with a proposal in order to resolve the problem.

# Toys

To replace traditional materials for toy production, his staff approached Lord Beaverbrook (publisher of the Daily Express at the time). It was in his interest that Woolworths kept their prices at just sixpence during the war. Woolworths produced and sold sets containing a cardboard boxing game pitting Winston Churchill against Adolf Hitler, Lumar patriotic jigsaw puzzles, and popular card games based on these terms. As the war progressed, these clever alternative toys became increasingly relevant since the toy industry was prohibited from using metal.

MONOPOLY

Did you Know?

The British Secret Intelligence commissioned John Waddington Ltd to develop a very unique version of the popular board game. Like in a spy film, real maps, compasses, and German money were hidden among objects POWs would find helpful in escaping. These items were distributed by a fake charity group.

World Events 1944

JAN

Leningrad siege ends

27th January. The 2 year siege finally ends. The last road to the city was cut off by the Wehrmacht on 8 September 1941. Red Army forces opened the city's land corridor on 18 January 1943, but the siege was not lifted until 27 January 1944, 872 days after it began. Due to the number of casualties sustained throughout the siege, the blockade became one of the longest and most destructive sieges in history.

Ban lifted

The national ban on married women teaching in Britain is lifted in March.

Solar eclipse

Jan 25th - In the Pacific Ocean, South America, the Atlantic Ocean, and Africa, a total solar eclipse took place during Solar Saros 130, the 48th solar eclipse.

"Big Week" begins

As part of the European strategic bombing campaign against Nazi Germany, the United States Army Air Forces and RAF Bomber Command conducted a series of raids from 20 to 25 February 1944, known as Big Week or Operation Argument. German aircraft were to be attacked to lure the Luftwaffe into a decisive battle where the Air Force could be crippled enough for the Allies to achieve air superiority, which would guarantee the success of the invasion of continental Europe.

Human Events

First issue of Human events is published (February) in Washington D.C

World events

Academy Award

The 16th Academy Awards Ceremony takes place at Grauman's Chinese Theatre in Hollywood, the first ever to take place at such a large public venue. Best Picture goes to Casablanca, directed by Michael Curtiz.

GI Bill of rights

On June 22nd, Franklin D. Roosevelt signs into law the GI Bill of Rights.

Enigma

The German navy's Enigma messages are decoded in England almost in real time.

Mahatma Ghandi

The Indian independence activist and leader Mahatma Gandhi was released from prison in May. As World War II raged, Gandhi encouraged civil unrest and uprisings against the British. An assassination attempt on his life was made not long after he was released. As a 78-year-old man, Gandhi lived to see India achieve independence in August of 1947 but was assassinated less than a year later in January of 1948.

Hans Aspergers

June - Hans Asperger publishes his paper on Asperger syndrome.

World Events 1944

SEP

Operation Market Garden

As the Battle of Arnhem (Operation Market Garden) begins on September 17th, Allied troops attempt the largest airborne military operation in history (at the time). This operation was intended to take bridges near the Rhine from the Germans by Allied paratroopers landing in the Netherlands. A successful push through Germany would have ended the war much more quickly if Allied troops were successful.

German troops had advanced notice of the Allies' arrival, so they were able to organise against them and destroy many of the bridges before the paratroopers landed. After reaching the Arnhem bridge, some Allied forces abandoned their plans due to a lack of supplies, leaving Germany in control of the Rhine.

Philippines Battle of Leyte Gulf

The Battle of Leyte Gulf occurs in October. Known as one of the largest naval battles in history, the main battle was fought between October 23rd and 26th. The invasion of the Japanese-occupied Philippines began by landing in the Leyte Gulf by American, Australian, and Filipino forces. As a result, the Japanese navy suffered heavy losses and kamikaze attacks took place for the first time. It was the Allies' victory that led to the Philippines' liberation. As a result, Japan was effectively cut off from its supply route in Southeast Asia and experienced a devastating loss in naval forces with thousands of ships destroyed.

King George II of Greece

King George II of Greece declares a regency, leaving his throne vacant.

World events

Battle of the Bulge

As Allied armies traveled through the Ardennes in December, the Germans attempted to surprise them. In a surprise attack, the Germans hoped to split the Allies up. December 16th marked the beginning of the battle, which continued until late January 1945. The line of defence of the Allies formed the shape of a bulge as the Allies regrouped to fight back against the German attack. This battle was the bloodiest for the United States during World War II, as it caught the Allies off guard and resulted in tens of thousands of deaths (estimated up to 100,000 casualties) during fierce fighting. The German offensive was stopped and Antwerp was not retaken by the Germans

V2 Rocket

First V2 rocket strikes London.

Iceland

Iceland declares full independence from Denmark. In February, Iceland is founded as a republic. A referendum was proposed by the Icelandic parliament to decide the nation's future after Iceland severed ties with Denmark. It was decided in May of that year to sever ties with Denmark and establish a republic by a surprisingly large majority. The turnout was 98 percent, and over 90 percent voted in favour of both criteria. In June, when Sveinn Bjornsson became the country's first president, the country celebrated its official independence.

Inventions from the early 40s

It is widely believed that the 1940s were one of the most important decades of the past century. As a direct result of the war, technology was born that would change our lives forever. Inventions that resulted from the events of the 1940s still have an impact on society today.

First patented in 1927, the aerosol concept dates back to the 1790s, but it wasn't until 1941 that Lyle Goodhue & William Sullivan applied it to efficient use. They have been widely credited as being the inventors of the modern spray can. This method was invented during WWII to kill malaria-carrying bugs.

Biomimicry

Velcro

This is a fascinating story of inspiration. De Mentral noticed how effective the burrs were at attaching themselves to his dogs while walking with them. As a result of his flash of inspiration, he came up with velcro, a material that has countless uses.

A system developed by CBS and Peter Goldmark transmitted images in all three primary colours. John Logie Baird's designs were used in designing their TV.

Mobile phones

Is it surprising? In 1947, T&T proposed the allocation of radio-spectrum frequencies with the intention of providing widespread telephone service, decades before the first commercially viable phone became available in 1983. Using police car technology, Bell Laboratories introduced the idea of cellular communications in 1947.

The Jeep

Karl Probst designed it in just 18 hours in 1940. In just 72 days, the first prototype was produced

The Z3 was the world's first fully automatic, programmable digital computer, invented by Konrad Zuse on May 12th 1941. Furthermore, it was the first computer controlled by software. The computer had 2,600 relays and operated at approximately 4-5 Hz with a 22-bit word

Inventions from the early 40s

Atomic Bomb

"I am become Death, the destroyer of worlds." The words that theoretical physicist, Herman Oppenheimer reportedly wrote after seeing the results of his invention. This quote is from a Hindu scripture that is also said to have been mistranslated. The atomic bomb and its destructive power had a profound impact on the course of WWII, the coming Cold War, and our history.

The Kidney Dialysis Machine

As a pioneer in hemodialysis and artificial organs, Willem Johan Pim Kolff made a significant contribution to both fields. He made major discoveries in kidney dialysis during WWII, which saved countless lives.

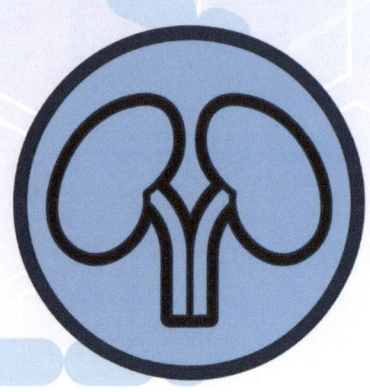

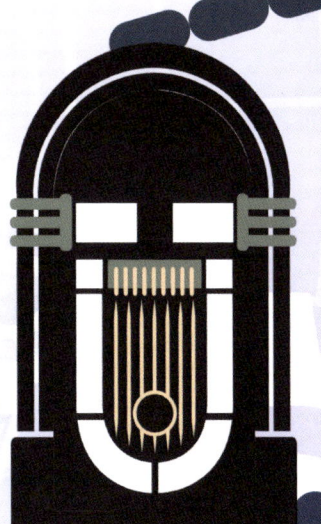

The Juke Box

It was during the 1890s that the first jukebox was put into play, but jukeboxes as we know them today did not appear until the 1940s. Jukeboxes were so popular in the 1940's that it is estimated two thirds of all records were played on them.

Microwave

The microwave was invented in 1947 by Percy Spence. In fact, the invention was based on radar technology developed during the war. However, even so, it was still far from what we know today as a microwave. It wasn't until 1967 that the countertop-friendly microwave was introduced.

Evacuation

As evacuees, many British children lived with host families during 1941. Approximately 3.5 million children were evacuated by the end of the war.

Evacuations began in 1939 and continued for three rounds. As the bombings did not occur immediately, the children returned home.

Children were again sent away for safety during the autumn 1940 blitz. Women who were pregnant were also evacuated - many babies were born in the countryside and returned to the city after the danger had passed.

Loose Lips Sink Ships

Advertising and propaganda during World War II.

The government reused many of the WWI campaigns. It was possible to persuade the British public to support a variety of different requests using some of the most effective posters. Messages used in propaganda to win the war promoted pro-war projects, fostered hostility against Hitler, encouraged evacuations and volunteer activities, and bolstered support for the allies. The message that Hitler was just around the corner and everyone had a role to play was effectively communicated through print, radio, and cinema advertising. There were patriotic 'you can do your part' messages mixed with fear-inducing messages.

Ministry of Food's Dig For Victory campaign

In 1939, only 30% of the food consumed in Britain was grown on British soil. Food imports were already common in the country. In order to ensure the nation's food security, the dig for victory campaign and the grow your own campaign were essential. A whopping tonne of vegetables were produced per year on over 1.4 million allotments by 1941.

The art of making do and mend

Clothing rationing began in June 1941. An advertising campaign followed that encouraged people to be resourceful. The Board of Trade launched the Make Do and Mend campaign. People were encouraged to adapt their existing wardrobes instead of buying new ones. Artists designed visually appealing and clear posters.

The Blitz

World War II's 'Blitz' was a relentless bombardment of London and other cities. A continuous bombing campaign lasted from late 1940 to spring 1941. A large number of cities, ports, and industrial areas were bombed by the Germans.

Over the course of 11 weeks, London was the prime target and was attacked every day and night. A third of London was destroyed. Additionally, terrible attacks took place in Swansea, Cardiff, Bristol, Southampton, Plymouth, Birmingham, Coventry, and Liverpool. During a raid on Coventry in November 1940, 4,330 homes were destroyed and 554 people were killed.

The V Campaign

During the darkest days of World War Two, this famous symbol boosted British morale. Churchill made the V for Victory hand gesture one of the most recognisable images of the war.

When the gesture, now called 'peace,' was made in 1941, it had a much greater impact than it does now. Although Churchill is synonymous with the wartime symbol, he did not come up with it.

Initially used in Belgium, the powerful sign spread across Europe and then to Britain a year later. Churchill used the V for Victory sign for the first time on July 19, 1941.

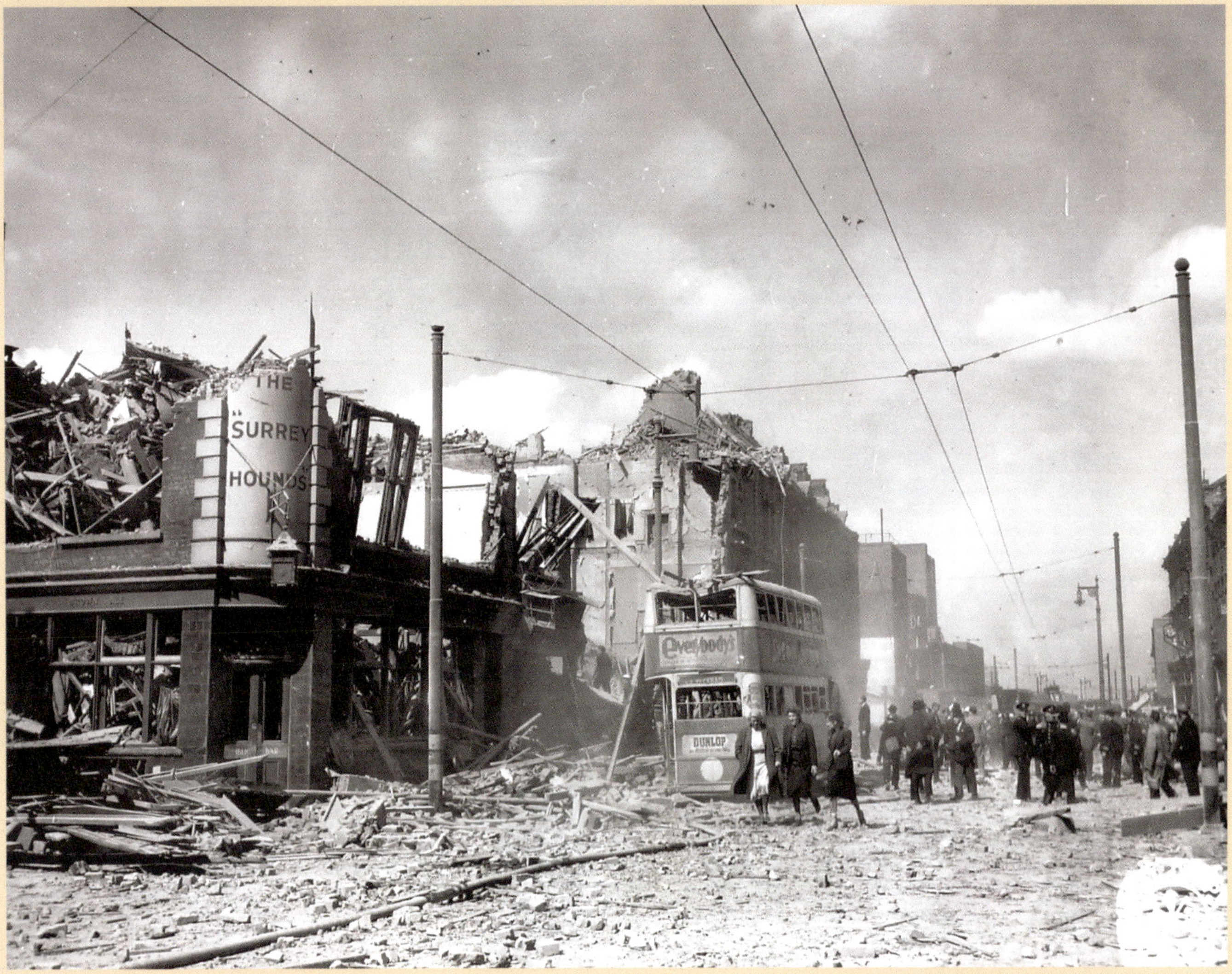
THE
SURREY
HOUNDS
DUNLOP

They use me on the kitchen front
Cautionary Tale!

DIG FOR VICTORY

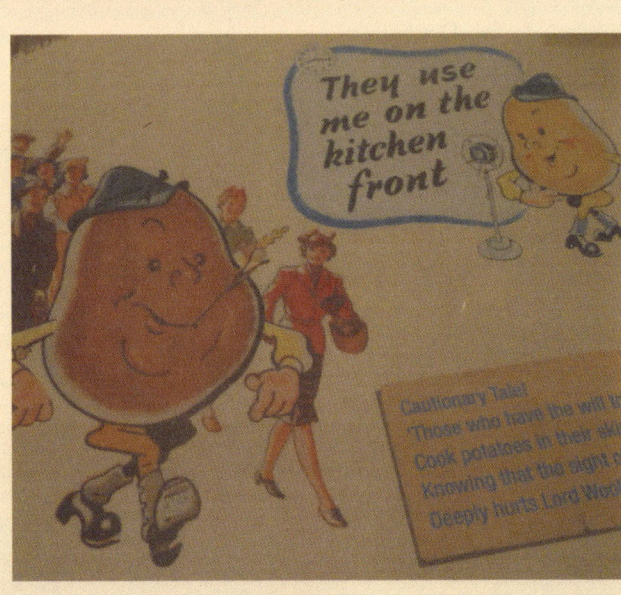

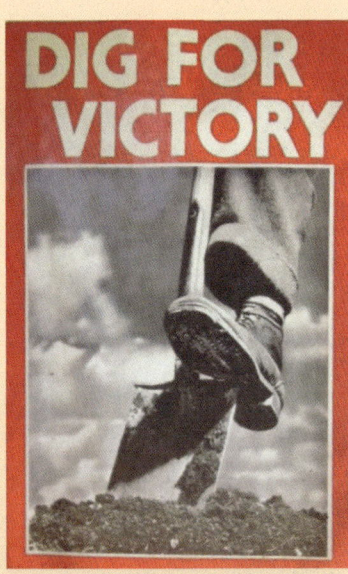

CITY OF LONDON POLICE
DANGER
UNEXPLODED BOMB

BETTER POT-LUCK with Churchill today **THAN HUMBLE PIE** under Hitler tomorrow
DON'T WASTE FOOD!

Beat 'FIREBOMB FRITZ'
BRITAIN SHALL NOT BURN

PUBLIC SHELTERS IN VAULTS UNDER PAVEMENTS IN THIS STREET

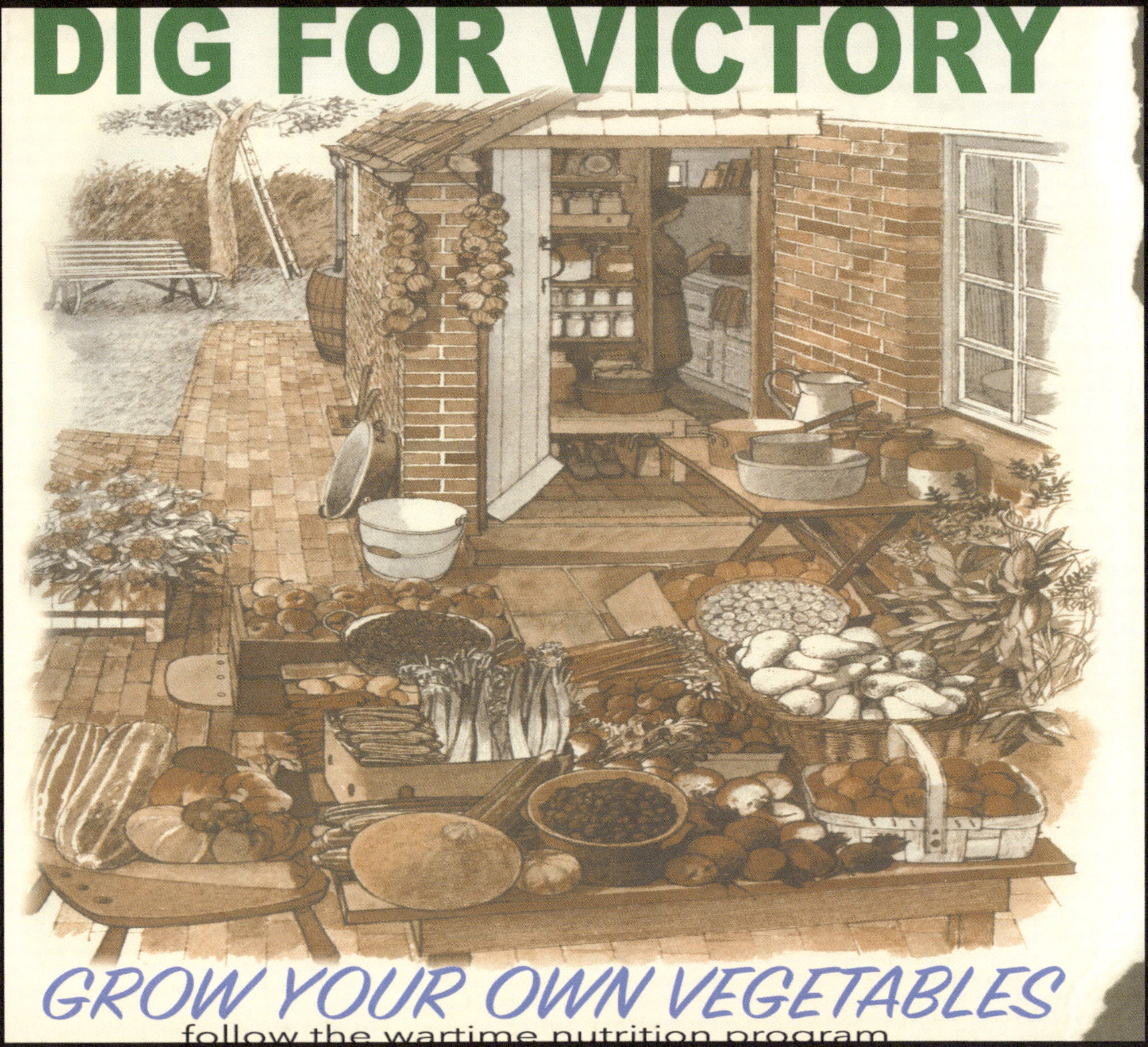
DIG FOR VICTORY
GROW YOUR OWN VEGETABLES
follow the wartime nutrition program

UNDERGROUND
THIS WAY
TO THE
AIR RAID SHELTER
WESTON STREET SE1
LONDON BOROUGH OF SOUTHWARK

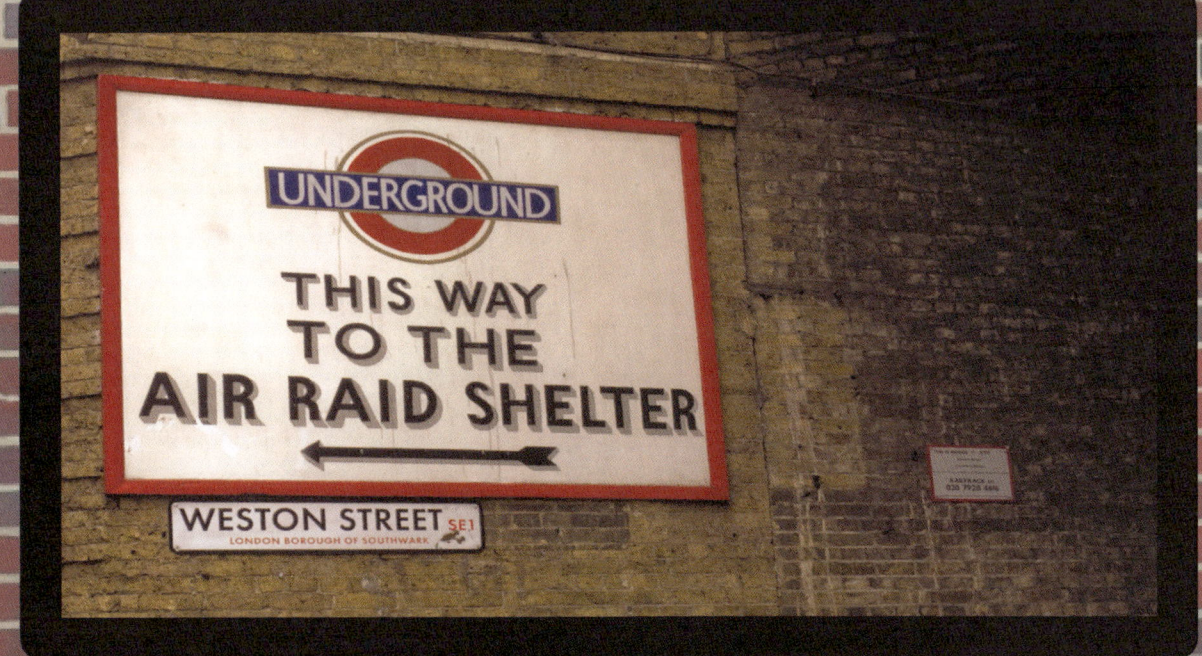

The legal stuff

All rights reserved @ Little Pips Press

2024

Attribution for photo images goes to the following talented photographers under the creative commons licenses specified:

Attribution 4.0 International (CC BY 4.0)
Attribution-ShareAlike 4.0 International (CC BY-SA 4.0)

Various photo images are licensed under the following https://creativecommons.org/licenses/by/2.0

www.flickr.com/photos/bongonian/8720834120

www.flickr.com/photos/wainwell7XrQWU-bDU2sK-bqZ5PA-bE8L5K-c16mgY-brdRCf-bE8N52-brdUrQ-c16tWy-brdQrW-brdQaf

https://www.flickr.com/photos/67331818@N03/8435815214

https://www.flickr.com/photos/39415781@N06/5121548642

https://www.flickr.com/photo25797459@N06/3255446185

https://www.flickr.com/photos/28884294@N04/4397471133

https://www.flickr.com/photos/37996637875@N01/1129554100

https://commons.wikimedia.org/index.php?curid=50788264

https://www.flickr.com/photos/47201412@N02/6634268777

https://www.flickr.com/photos/41525293@N00/4488405042

https://www.flickr.com/photos/39735679@N00/443628643

ttps://www.flickr.com/photos/24592131@N00/32399988

https://www.flickr.com/photos/hotzeplotz/67495932/in/gallery-189870699@N02-72157715884590167

https://www.flickr.com/photos/repolco/46431567025/in/gallery-189870699@N02-72157715884590167

https://www.flickr.com/photos/levanrami/44709621625/in/gallery-189870699@N02-72157715884590167

https://www.flickr.com/photos/156515782@N02/49604265887/in/gallery-189870699@N02-72157715884590167

https://www.flickr.com/photos/christopherdombres/5397965371/in/gallery-189870699@N02-72157715884590167

https://www.flickr.com/photos/10413717@N08/4548816970/in/gallery-189870699@N02-72157715884590167

https://www.flickr.com/photos/charlottehenard/8296290551/in/gallery-189870699@N02-72157715884590167

https://www.flickr.com/photos/dave_fisher/4841419011/in/gallery-189870699@N02-72157715884590167

https://www.flickr.com/photos/97534175@N00/5489867060/in/gallery-189870699@N02-72157715884590167/

https://www.flickr.com/photos/97534175@N00/5489868202/in/gallery-189870699@N02-72157715884590167/

https://www.flickr.com/photos/88010770@N05/33731941188/in/gallery-189870699@N02-72157715884590167

https://www.flickr.com/photos/156515782@N02/38969849552/in/gallery-189870699@N02-72157715884590167/

https://www.flickr.com/photos/anthonymason/17353582065/in/gallery-189870699@N02-72157715884590167

https://www.flickr.com/photos/fylin/387596912/in/gallery-189870699@N02-72157715884590167

https://www.flickr.com/photos/dedrawolf
"Identity and Ration Books" by HerryLawford is licensed under CC BY 2.0.

https://www.flickr.com/photos/hansthijs/3620270045/in/photolist

Printed in Great Britain
by Amazon